The finest Legends of the Rhine

The finest Legends
of the Rhine

by

Wilhelm Ruland

Verlag von Hoursch & Bechstedt in Köln⌀E.

The publishers desire to thank Mr. Andrew Mitchell and Mr. H. J. Findlay, Edinburgh, for valuable assistance in the preparation of the new English edition.

Worms

The Nibelungen Song

To-day we are deeply touched, as our fore-fathers must have been, at the recital of the boundless suffering and the overwhelming con-catenation of sin and expiation in the lives of the Recken and Frauen of the Nibelungen Legend. That naive singer has remained name-less and unknown, who about the end of the 12th century wrote down this legend in poetic form, thus preserving forever our most precious relic of Germanic Folksepic. A powerful story it is of sin and suffering: corresponding to the world itself and just as the primitive mind of a people loves to represent it. The story begins as a lovely idyll but ends in gloomy tragedy.

The ancient Rhenish town of Worms was during the great migrations the seat of authority of the Burgundian invaders, an east Germanic stock. During the glorious reign of King Gunther there appears, attracted by the beauty of Chriemhild the king's sister, a young hero, Siegfried, by name. He is himself a king's son, his father Siegmund reigning in Xanten „nieden by dem Rine". King Gunther receives the fair Recken into his service as a vassal.

Siegfried, exhibiting the fairest loyalty to his overlord, and rendered invisible by magic, conquers for him the redoubtable Brunhild, the proud queen of the island kingdom of Isenland (Iceland) and compels her to wed King Gunther. As a reward Siegfried receives the hand of Chriemhild. In the fulness of his heart the hero presents to Chriemhild as a marriage gift, the Nibelungen Hoard, which he had gained in his early years from the sons of the king of the Nibelungen and from Dwarf Alberich the guardian of the treasure.

Joy reigns in the king's court at Worms, but it was not shared by all. Besides Chriemhild there was another secretly drawn towards the hero, and in Brunhild's heart the bridal happiness of Chriemhild awakens such envy that soon no friendly word passes between the women. They become estranged and one day her bad feeling leads Brunhild to harsh words. Then alas, Chriemhild gave unbridled licence to her tongue. In her rash insolence she represents to Brunhild that it was not Gunther but Siegfried who formerly overcame her. As proof of this she produces the ring and girdle which Siegfried had taken on that night from the powerful Brunhild, and which he had presented to Chriemhild. With fierce haughtiness Chriemhild taunts her opponent with a hateful name no

woman could endure, and forbids her to enter the cathedral.

Brunhild, weeping, informs King Gunther of the contumely heaped upon her. The king is filled with wrath, and his vassal, the gloomy Hagen considers how he may destroy Siegfried avowedly to avenge the Queen, but secretly for the possession of the Nibelungen Hoard. During a hunt in the Odenwald Siegfried was treacherously stabbed by Hagen whilst stooping to drink from a well. The intention was to spread the report that Siegfried had been slain by robbers whilst hunting alone. So, on the following day they crossed the Rhine back to Worms.

In the night Hagen caused the dead body of Siegfried to be laid in front of Chriemhild's chamber. In the early morning as Chriemhild accompanied by her attendants was preparing to go to mass in the cathedral she noticed the corpse of her hero. A wail of sorrow arose. Chriemhild threw herself weeping on the body of her murdered husband. "Alas!" she cried "thy shield is not hewn by swords: thou hast been foully murdered. Did I but know who has done this, I would avenge thy death." Chriemhild ordered a magnificent bier for her royal hero, and demanded that an ordeal should be held over the corpse. "For it is a marvellous thing, and to this day it happens, that when the bloodstained murderer approaches wounds bleed anew."

So all the princes and nobles of Burgundy walked past the dead body, above which was the figure of the crucified Redeemer of the world, and lo! when the grim Hagen came forward the wounds of the dead man began to flow. In the presence of the astounded men and horrified women Chriemhild accused Hagen of the assassination of her husband.

Much treachery and woe accompanied the expiation of this great crime. The Nibelungen Hoard, the cause of the shameful deed, was sunk in the middle of the Rhine*) in order to prevent future strife arising from human greed. But Chriemhild's undying sorrow was not mitigated, nor her unconquerable thirst for revenge appeased.

After the burial of his son King Siegmund begged in vain that Chriemhild should come to the royal city of Xanten; she remained at Worms for thirteen years constantly near her beloved dead.

Then the sorrowing woman removed to the Abbey of Lorch which her mother, Frau Ute, had founded. Thither also, she transferred Siegfried's body.

---

*) See cover picture

When Etzel (Attila) the ruler of the Huns wooed her, Chriemhild urged not by love but by very different feelings gave him her hand and accompanied her heathen lord to the Ungarnland. Then she treacherously invited Siegfried's murderers to visit her husband, and prepared for them a destruction which fills the mind with horror. The Burgundian king and his followers, who, since the Hoard had come into their possession, were called the Nibelungen, fell slaughtered in the Etzelburg under the swords of the Huns and their allies, thus atoning for their faithlessness to the hero Siegfried. And with this awful holocaust ends the Song of the Nibelungen Not, the most renowned heroic legend in the German tongue.

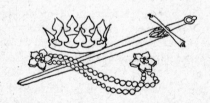

Mayence

Heinrich Frauenlob

The priest or as some say, canon, in the old town of Mayence was a very worthy man, and at the same time a heaven-gifted singer. Besides devoting himself to science, he composed numerous pious verses which he dedicated to the Holy Virgin. He also played the harp, and wrote many beautiful songs in honour of the female sex.

In contrast to many contemporary poets, he considered "woman" a higher title than "wife" which only signifies a married woman. So on account of the chivalry displayed in his numberless poems and songs, posterity gave him the name of "Frauenlob", under which title he is better known than under his own name of Heinrich of Meissen.

The love and veneration which thankful women paid him was very great, not only during his life-time, but even more so after his death. Their grief was intense when it became known that the poet's voice would never more be heard in this world. It was agreed to honour him with such a burial as no poet had ever before received. The funeral procession moved slowly and sorrowfully along the streets, the greater part of the cortege being women in deep mourning who prayed for the repose of the poet's soul. Eight of the most beautiful among them carried the coffin, which was covered with sweet-scented flowers.

At the grave songs of lamentation were heard from women's gentle voices. Precious Rhine-wine which had been the poet's favourite drink, and which so often had inspired his poetry, was poured by hands of his admirers over his grave, so profusely, the legend relates, that the entrance of the church was flooded by the libation. But still more precious than all these gifts were the tears, which on this memorable day were shed by many a gentle lady.

The wanderer can still see the monument erected to this great benefactor in the cathedral at Mayence, which represents the figure of a beautiful woman in pure-white marble placing a wreath on the coffin of the great singer, who had honoured women in the most chivalrous of songs.

Bishop Willigis

In the year 1000 there was a very pious priest in Mayence called Bishop Willigis. He was only the son of a poor wheelwright, but by his perseverance and his own merit he had attained to the dignity of first priest of the kingdom. The honest citizens of Mayence loved and honoured the worthy divine, although they did not altogether like having to bow down to one who had been brought up in a simple cottage like themselves.

The bishop once reproved them in gentle tones for thinking too much of mere descent. This vexed the supercilious citizens, and one night they determined to play Willigis a trick. They took some chalk and drew enormous wheels on all the doors of his house.

Early next morning as the bishop was going to mass, he noticed the scoffers' malicious work. He stood silently looking at the wheels, the chaplain by his side expecting every moment that the reverend prelate would burst forth in a terrible rage. But a gay smile spread over the bishop's features, and ordering a painter to be sent to him, he told him to paint white wheels on a scarlet background, visible to every eye, just where the chalk wheels had been drawn, and unerneath to paint the words,

"Willigis! Willigis! just think what you have risen from." But he did not stop there. He ordered the wheelwright to make him a plough-wheel, and caused it to be placed over his couch in memory of his extraction.

Thereafter the scoffers were put to silence, and the people of Mayence began to honour and esteem their worthy bishop, who, though he had been so exalted, possessed such honest common-sense.

White wheels on a red ground have been the arms of the Bishops of Mayence ever since.

Ingelheim

Eginhard and Emma

I.

The story which we have now to relate is a very touching one, and it becomes even more interesting when we know that it is based on real fact.

In the little town of Ingelheim there was a beautiful marble castle, the favourite residence of Charlemagne. He often retired to this lonely, peaceful spot accompanied only by a few of his faithful vassals and the members of his own family. Eginhard, the emperor's private secretary, was never missing from this little circle. Charlemagne thought highly of this man, then in the prime of youth, on account of his profound knowledge and extraordinary talents.

The young scholar, so different from the wise councillors not only in his learning but in his cultivated manners, was a great favourite among the ladies of the court.

Eginhard who was a constant companion of the emperor, had also become an intimate member of the family circle, and Charlemagne entrusted him with the education of his favourite child Emma, daughter of his wife Gismonda. This dark-eyed maiden was considered the most beautiful of her age, and the young scholar could not long remain cold and indifferent to her charms. The undisturbed hours which should have been spent in learning, led to a mutual understanding. Eginhard struggled to remind himself of his duty towards his sovereign, but love overcame him, and soon an oath of eternal fidelity united these young hearts.

II.

The great emperor ought to have known what would be the consequence of allowing the young scholar to enjoy the society of his dark-eyed, passionate daughter. In the still hours of the night when all the inmates of the castle lay wrapped in sleep, Eginhard sought the chamber of his beloved. She listened enchanted to the glowing words of his burning heart, but their love was chaste and pure, no gusts of passion troubling them.

But fate was against these lovers. One night they were sitting in Emma's chamber talking confidentially together. The great palace was veiled in darkness, no ray of light, no star was to be seen in the heavens. As Eginhard was about to leave the chamber, he perceived that the courtyard below was covered with snow. It would have been impossible to pass across it without leaving a trace behind him, but at all risks he must reach his room.

What was to be done? Love is ingenious. After considering for some time together, they both concluded that there was but one way to prevent their being betrayed. The slender maiden took her lover on her back and carried him across the courtyard, thus leaving behind only her small footprints.

It happened that Charles the Great had not yet sought the repose he needed so much, as care banished sleep from his eyes. He sat at his window and looked out into the silent night. In the courtyard below he perceived a shadow crossing the pavement and, looking carefully, he recognised his favourite daughter Emma carrying a man on her back. — Yes! and this man was Eginhard his great favourite. Pain and anger struggled in his heart. He wanted to rush down and kill him — an emperor's daughter and a mere secretary — but with a great effort he restrained himself, mastered the violent agitation which this unexpected sight caused him, and went back to his chamber to wait wearily for dawn.

III.

The next day Charles assembled his councillors. They were all horrified to see his ghastly look; his brow was dark, and sorrow was depicted on every feature. Eginhard looked

at his master apprehending coming evil.
Charlemagne stood up and spoke: —

"What does a royal princess deserve, who
receives the visit of a man at night?" The
councillors looked at each other speechless.
Eginhard's countenance became white as death.
The councillors soon guessed the name of the
royal princess, and they consulted together for
some time not knowing what to say, but at last
one councillor answered: —

"Your Majesty, we think that a weak woman
must not be punished for anything done out
of love."

"And what does a favourite of the emperor
deserve who creeps into a royal princess'
chamber at night?"

Charlemagne cast a dark look at his secretary,
who trembled and became even paler. "Alas!
all is lost", murmured he to himself. Then,
raising his voice, he said, "Death, my Master
and Emperor!"

Charles looked at the young man full of
astonishment. The wrath in his soul melted at
this self-accusation and fervent repentance.
Deep silence followed this answer, and in a few
minutes the emperor dismissed his councillors,
making a sign at the same time to Eginhard to
follow him.

Without a word Charles led him into his private chamber, where in answer to his summons, Emma appeared.

Her heart misgave her as she saw the dark look on her father's face and the troubled features of her beloved. She understood all at once, and with a convulsive cry of pain threw herself at her father's feet.

„Mercy! mercy! my father, we love each other so dearly!" murmured she, raising her large eyes imploringly. "Mercy!" murmured Eginhard too, bending his knees.

The emperor remained silent. After a time he began to speak earnestly and coldly at first, but his voice changed to a milder tone on hearing the sobs of his favourite child.

"I shall not separate you who are bound to each other by love. A priest shall unite you, and at dawn to-morrow you must both be gone from the castle, never to return."

He left them, shutting the door behind him.

The beautiful maiden sank down on her knees, only half conscious in her grief of what her father had said. But Eginhard's soft voice soon whispered in her ear.

"Do not weep, Emma. By thrusting you from him, your father, my master, has only bound us together for ever. Come," he continued in a trembling voice, alarmed at her passionate tears, "we must go, but love will be ever with us."

The next day two pilgrims left the castle of Ingelheim, and took the road in the direction of Mayence.

IV.

Time wore on.

Charles the Great had made war on Saxony, had set the Roman crown upon his own head, and had become famous throughout the whole world. But all his fame had not prevented his hair from becoming grey, nor his heart from being sad. A mournful picture hat imprinted itself on his mind, despite all his efforts to forget the past. In the evening when the setting sun glittered on the marble pillars of the royal palace, casting its golden rays into the chamber of the great emperor, it would find him sitting motionless in his carved oak-chair, his grey head buried in his hands, mournful dreams troubling his peace. He was thinking of the days which were past, of the young man whose gentle ways made him so different from the rough warriors of the court, how he used to recite poetry and sing the songs of the old bards so passionately, and the old legends, which the emperor prized so much, how he used to read to him from the old gray parchment which he, Eginhard, had written so carefully, how his own favourite dark-eyed daughter had so often been present, sitting at his feet listening intently to the reader — all this came back to his memory, saddening his heart, and filling his eyes with tears.

V.

Bugle-horns sounded through the forest, Charles and his followers were at the chase. The old emperor, seeking to forget his grief, had seized his spear and had gone out to hunt.

In his eagerness to follow a magnificent stag he had become separated from his escort. The sun was already low in the west; the animal, now seeing no way of escape, as his pursuer was close behind him, dashed into a river and swam to the other side. The emperor, in hot pursuit and much exhausted, arrived at the water's edge, and for the first time noticed that he was alone, and in a part of the country quite unknown to him.

The river lay before him and the forest behind, but the latter seemed to be quite impenetrable. It was already night, and Charles sought in vain to find some path or track.

As he was looking round him, he perceived a light in the distance. Greatly pleased he started off in that direction, and found a little hut close to the river, but on looking through the window Charlemagne saw that the room was a very poor one.

"Perhaps this is the hermitage of some pious man," thought he, and knocked at the door, whereupon a fair haired man appeared on the threshold.

Without mentioning his name, the emperor informed him what had happened, and begged shelter for the night.

At the sound of this loved voice, the man trembled, but controlling himself, he invited the emperor to enter. A young woman was sitting on a stool rocking a baby in her arms. She started, became very pale at the sight of the emperor, and then hurried into the next room to hide her emotion; Charles sat down, and refusing refreshment from his host leaned his head wearily on his hands.

Minutes passed, and still he sat there lost in thought, dreaming of those happy by-gone days.

At last the sweet prattle of a child roused him, and looking up he saw a little girl about five years old at his side, stretching out her arms to him, bidding him good-night. Charles looked closely at the little angel-like creature, his heart throbbing within him. "What is your name, little one?" asked he. "Emma," answered the child.

"Emma," repeated Charles with tears in his eyes, and drawing the child closer to him he pressed a kiss on its forehead.

In a moment the man and his young wife were at the emperor's feet imploring pardon. "Emma! Eginhard!" cried he with great emotion, embracing them both. "Blessed be the place where I have found you again!"

*

Emma and Eginhard returned in great pomp to the emperor's court. The latter gave them his beautiful palace at Ingelheim, and only felt himself happy when he was with them.

He caused a cloister to be built on the spot where he had found them again, which, to the present day is called "Seligenstadt", "town of the happy".

In the church belonging to this little town the tomb of Eginhard and Emma is still shown, for according to their wishes, their bones were interred in same coffin.

Johannisberg

Wherever the German tongue is heard, and even further still, the king of all Rhine wines, "Johannisberger" is known and sought after. Every friend of the grape which grows on the banks of this river is well acquainted with it, but few perhaps know of its princely origin. It is princely, not because princes' hands once kept the key to Johannisberg, but rather because princely hands planted the vine in the Rhine country, and this royal giver was no other than Charlemagne, the all-powerful ruler of the kingdom of the Franks.

Once in early spring Charles the Great was standing on the balcony of his castle at Ingelheim, his eyes straying over the beautiful stretch of country at his feet. Snow had fallen during the night, and the hills of Rüdesheim were clothed in white. As the imperial ruler was looking thoughtfully over the landscape, he noticed that the snow on one side of Johannisberg melted quicker in the sun's rays than on any other part. Charles, who was a great and deep thinker, began to reflect that on a spot where the rays of the sun shone so genially, something better than grass would thrive.

Sending for Kunrat his faithful servant, he bade him saddle his horse the next day at

dawn and ride to Orleans, a town famous for its good wine. He was to inform the citizens that the emperor had not forgotten the excellent wine they had given him there, and that he would like to grow the same vines on the Rhine. He desired the citizens of Orleans therefore to send him plants from their country.

The messenger set off to do the king's bidding and ere the moon had again gone round her course, was back in the castle at Ingelheim. Great satisfaction prevailed at court. Charles, mighty ruler as he was, even went so far as to cross to Rüdesheim, where he planted with his royal hand the French vine in German soil.

This was no mere passing whim on the part of the emperor. He sent messengers constantly to bring word how the vines were thriving in Rüdesheim and on the flanks of Johannisberg, and when the third autumn had come round, the Emperor Charlemagne set out from his favourite resort, Aix-la-Chapelle, for the Rhine country, and great rejoicing prevailed among the vine-reapers from Rüdesheim to Johannisberg.

The first cup of wine was solemnly offered to the emperor, a golden wine in a golden goblet, a wine worthy of a king.

Charles took a long deep draught, and with brightened eyes praised the delicous drink. It became his favourite wine, this fiery "Johannisberger", making him young again in his old age. What Charlemagne then felt when he drank this wine, every one who raises the sparkling grapejuice to his lips is keenly sensible of also. Wherever the German tongue is heard, and even further still, the king of all Rhine wines is known and sought after, Johannisberger wine.

The legend weaves another wonderful tale about the great emperor blessing his grapes.

A poet's pen has fashioned it into a song, which is still often heard among the grapegatherers.

Every spring when the vines are blossoming on the hills and in the valleys along the river, and their fragrance scents the air, a tall shadow wanders about the vineyards at night, a purple mantle hanging from his stately shoulders, and a crown on his head. It is Charlemagne, the great Emperor, who planted the grapes long years before. The luscious scent of the blossoms wakens him up from his tomb in Aix-la-Chapelle, and he comes to bless the grapes.

When the full moon gently casts her bright beams on the water, lighting up the emperor's nightly path, he may be seen crossing the golden bridge formed by her rays and then wandering further along the hills, blessing the vines on the other side of the river.

At the first crow of the cock he returns to his grave in Aix-la-Chapelle, and sleeps till the scent of the grapes wakens him next spring, when he again wanders through the countries along the Rhine, blessing the vineyards.

Bingen

The Mouse-Tower

Below Bingen in the middle of the Rhine there is a lonely island on which a stronghold is to be seen. This tower is called "the Mouse-Tower". For many centuries a very gloomy tale has been told about it in connection with Hatto, Archbishop op Mayence, whose evil deeds were well-known throughout the country.

Hatto is said to have been ambitious, heartless, and perfidious, as well as cruel towards the poor. He extorted taxes from his people, tolls were imposed, and new burdens invented only to gratify his haughty pride and his love of display. On a little island between Bingen and Rüdesheim he caused a tower to be built, so that all passing ships could be stopped in the narrow passage, where they were obliged to pay toll.

Soon after the building of this customhouse there was a very bad harvest in the country round Mayence. Drought had parched the fields, and the little seed remaining had been destroyed by hail. The scarcity was felt all the more, because the bishop had bought up all the stores of corn that were left from the year

31

before, and had stored them up safely in his granaries.

A terrible famine now threatened the land, spreading misery among the poor. The unhappy people implored the cruel bishop to lower the price of the corn in his store-house, which he wished to sell at such exorbitant prices that his subjects could not buy it. All their petitions were in vain. His advisers besought him to have pity on the deplorable condition of the poor, but Hatto remained unmoved. When cries of distress and the murmuring voices of the exasperated folk were raised against their hard-hearted master, the bishop gave free vent to the wicked thoughts of his soul.

One day a troop of hungry beggars came crowding to the episcopal palace crying for food. Hatto and his guests were just sitting down to a luxurious banquet. The bishop had been talking to his companions of these wretched people, and had expressed his opinion that it would be a good thing to do away with them altogether in some drastic way.

As the ragged mob of men, women, and children, with hollow cheeks and pale faces threw themselves at his feet crying for bread, a still more fiendish plan suggested itself. Beckoning to them with hypocritical kindness he promised them corn, and caused them to be

led outside the town to a barn, where each one was to receive as much corn as he wished. The unhappy folk hurried forth, their hearts full of gratitude; but when they were all in the barn, Hatto ordered the doors to be locked and the barn to be set on fire.

The screams of the poor wretches were heart-rending, and could be heard even in the bishop's palace.

But cruel Hatto called out scornfully to his advisers, "Listen! how the mice are squeaking among the corn. This eternal begging is at an end at last. May the mice bite me if is not true!"

But the punishment which Heaven sent him was terrible. Thousands of mice came out of the burning barn, made their way to the palace, filled every chamber and corner, and at last attacked the bishop himself. His servants killed them by hundreds, but their numbers seemed only to increase, as did their ferocity also. The bishop was seized with horror and, anticipating God's punishment, he fled from the town and went on board a boat hoping to defend himself from his terrible pursuers. But the innumerable horde swam in legions after him, and when he reached his tower on the island thinking at least he would be safe there, the mice followed him, gnawing the tower and tearing for themselves an entrance with their sharp teeth, till at last they reached him whom they sought. The cruel man was devoured by the mice, which attacked him by scores. In his despair he offered his soul to the Evil One, if he would release his body from such awful agony. The Evil Spirit came, freed his body, but took his soul away for himself.

Thus runs the legend. History however speaks less severely of Hatto, the imperious prelate.

*

His great ambition was his desire of power. He was the founder of the temporal power which the seat of Mayence obtained, and which later on made it the first bishopric of the kingdom, but he was always hated by the citizens, who suffered much owing to his proud, despotic character.

It is true that he was the founder of the toll which ships in olden times were obliged to pay on the Rhine, so that this fact and many other cruel exactions of him, have helped to evolve the terrible legend of the Mouse-Tower.

Castle Rheinstein

The Wooing

In Castle Rheinstein once lived a knight called Diethelm, who devoted himself without restraint to all the excesses of the robber barons. From one of his pillaging expeditions he brought back a charming maiden called Jutta. As the delicate ivy twines itself round the rough oak and clothes its knotty stem with shimmering velvet, so in time the gentle conduct of this maiden changed the coarse baron to a noble knight who eschewed pillaging and carousing, and ultimately made the fair Jutta the honoured wife of her captor.

The first fruit of their love cost the tender mother her life. Gerda however, who much resembled her mother, grew to such a noble beauty that soon wooers from far and near came to sue for the hand of the beautiful daughter of the aged Diethelm. But the aged knight made a most careful selection, and many gay wooers had to depart in sorrow. One young man was however regarded favourably by the maid, and not unkindly looked upon by the old man. He was the oldest son of the owner of the Sternburg. This young man had contrived to win the maiden's heart, and one day, while

Gerda presided as queen of love and beauty at a tournament held in the courtyard of Castle Rheinstein, Helmbrecht made an avowal of his love.

Some days thereafter the young lord according to courtly fashion appointed his uncle Gunzelin of Reichenstein to woo his chosen bride for him. But Gunzelin though an old man was full of knavery and falsehood, and so instead of wooing for his nephew he ingratiated himself with Gerda's father. Moreover, as the old knight was descended from an ancient family and possessed of much wealth Diethelm was easily induced to promise him the hand of the fair Gerda. To the astonishment of this worthy pair Gerda would not listen to the suit of her rich wooer. Her heart belonged to the nephew, not the uncle. Now Count Diethelm was aroused, and with the blind fury of his earlier years swore to his rich companion that Gerda belonged to him, and should never wed the young cocksparrow of the Sternburg.

In her quiet chamber the unhappy maid wept out her heart's grief, but burning tears did not thaw the ice-cold heart of the father. In vain the young lover tried to gain the old knight's favour, but Diethelm merely referred to his knightly word solemnly pledged to the lord of Reichenstein.

Soon the day approached on which Gunzelin, with the smiling self satisfaction of an old roué, and decked out to give himself all the appearance of young manhood, was to lead the fairest maiden in the Rhineland to his stately castle. Gerda who possessed the mild disposition of her deceased mother had submitted to the inevitable. On a bright summer morning the bridal procession started from the courtyard of Castle Rheinstein, and moved towards the Clement's Chapel situated in the neighbourhood. Horns blew and trumpets sounded. On a milk-white palfrey, sat the fair young bride, deadly pale. She was thinking of her absent lover who in this hour must be enduring the greatest anguish on her account. Then all at once a swarm of buzzing gradflies came out of the bush and fastened fiercely on the palfrey which bore the fair Gerda. The animal reared and broke from the bridal procession. Boldly the bridegroom on his grandly caparisoned steed dashed forward to check the frightened animal, but his warhorse missing its footing on the narrow bridle path fell over a precipice carrying its master with it. The dying knight was carried by the wedding-guests back to Castle Rheinstein. The aged Diethelm was also unfortunate in his attempt to stop the runaway steed. The maddened animal had struck him on the shin-

bone, and wounded him. The servants were thus obliged to carry the moaning greybeard back to his castle as speedily and carefully as possible. The surgeon had a sad time of it during the next week as he attended to the enraged old knight's wounds and bruises.

When the runaway horse had disappeared round a bend of the path a man threw himself upon it, and bringing the trembling animal to a standstill clasped the unconscious bride in his arms. Helmbrecht, concealed in the brushwood, had been watching the bridal procession, and now came to the rescue of his true love. When the old lord heard of this he came to his senses and gave the lovers his blessing. Some weeks later a bridal procession advanced from the Clement's Chapel up to the festively decorated Castle Rheinstein. Trumpets were blown and horns resounded. Much more joyfully than on the previous occasion the musicians marched in front. Upon a milkwhite palfrey, as formerly, sat a noble maiden in bridal state, clothed in undulating robes bordered with fur. Her head was bent in maiden modesty as she listened to the endearments which the youthful knight whispered in her ear. Behind rode the father of the bride sunk in thought, and along with him was his pious sister Notburge, the canoness of Nonnenwerth.

A life of unalloyed married bliss followed this union, and God granted to the noble pair a long and happy life. They rest together in front of the altar in the Clement's Chapel which is situated across the Rhine from Assmannshausen. Burg Rheinstein has renewed its youth, and still from its precipitous height proudly over-looks the waters of our noble stream.

Castle Sooneck

The Blind Archer

In his stronghold at Sooneck, Siebold, one of
the most rapacious of the robber barons presided
over a godless revel. Wanton women with
showy apparel and painted cheeks lolled in the
arms of tipsy cavaliers. The music blared, and
to complete their carousal wine flowed freely.
The lord of Sooneck flushed with drinking, and
leering on the assembly with evil-looking eyes
spoke as follows:

"Noble ladies (drunken applause from his
worthy associates) and much-married nobles
(loudly giggled the shameless females), after
food and drink, I, as your host will be pleased
to entertain you by bringing before you a
ferocious animal which I keep confined here."

While the ladies pretended to take shelter
timidly behind their lords, and the men stared
at their host expecting some further expla-
nation, the doors of the room opened, and led
by two servants a man in coarse garments, and
with unkempt hair and beard stood before
them. A suppressed whisper passed round the
festive board and all eyes were fixed on the
haggard countenance of the prisoner. When for
a moment the weary eyelids were raised, two

ghastly cavities were visible. Again, with the same tone of levity, the lord of the castle spoke, "Lovely ladies, and knightly companions, the best marksman on the Rhine was Hans Veit of Fürsteneck. Like ourselves he was dreaded far and near. He and I entered on a feud of life and death. He went down."

"With broken and battered shield, bleeding from numerous wounds I lay prostrate before you awaiting manfully the death-thrust," murmured the prisoner, and his voice sounded as if from the grave. "It pained me to finish him off", said Siebold flippantly, "I got his two eyes taken out, and thus added to my collection of rarities, the best archer on the Rhine."

"My murdered eyes behold your scorn," said the prisoner harshly. "But surely chivalry still flourishes on Sooneck" said the lord of the castle. "Understand then that my servants have informed me, that even blind, you can, guided only by sounds, hit a given mark with a bolt. If you come out of this ordeal successful, freedom shall be the reward." Stormy applause greeted these words.

"Death were dearer to me than life," murmured the Blind Archer. As he seized the cross-bow however, a gleam of joy went over his countenance like a ray of sunshine over a sombre landscape. Crowded together in a corner

of the room the guests watched the proceedings.
The lord of Sooneck seized a goblet and ordered
the prisoner to draw upon it, after hearing the
sound. In the next moment the silver clang
resounded, as the goblet fell on the floor.

"Shoot now," said Siebold of Sooneck, and
immediately an arrow pierced his mouth. With
a grunt like a slaughtered ox, Siebold sank
among the rushes. Silent and motionless with
the two eye-cavities gaping, stood the blind
man. Then his shaggy head sank on his heaving
breast. Like a flock of frightened crows the
knights and their paramours fled, and only a
few terrified squires and servants muttered
prayers over the body of the lord of Sooneck.

Kaub

Castle Gutenfels

About the middle of the thirteenth century, there was a stately castle near Kaub which was inhabited by Count Philip of Falkenstein. There he lived very happily with his beautiful sister Guta, who was as good as she was fair.

Numerous knights had sought to win her love, but none had achieved this conquest, the castle maiden having no desire to exchange her brother's hospitable home for any other.

At that time a magnificent tournament was held at Cologne, to which knights from all countries of the kingdom far and near and even from England were invited.

A great multitude of spectators were assembled to see the stately knights contending for the prize, which a fair hand would bestow on them.

Among the nobles present at the tournament was a knight from England, whose graceful figure and splendid armour were particulary striking. He wore a veiled visor, and the stewards of the tournament announced him under the name of "the Lion Knight," a golden lion ornamenting his shield. Soon the majestic knight's master-like manner of fighting created a great sensation, and when he succeeded in unhorsing his opponent, a most formidable combatant, loud rejoicings rang through the lists.

Count Philip and his sister were among the guests. Guta had been watching the strange knight with ever increasing interest during the tournament, regretting at the same time that she could not see his face.

But an opportunity soon presented itself when the knight was declared victor. She was selected to present the prize, a golden laurel-wreath, to the winner, she became much embarrassed, and a feeling such as she had never before experienced seized her as she looked at the Briton's face for the first time.

Perhaps the knight may have read in the lovely maiden's countenance what she in vain tried to hide from him, perhaps a spark from that passionate fire which had so suddenly fired her heart, may have flown into his soul as he knelt before her to receive the wreath, which she placed on his head with a trembling hand. Who can tell?

Afterwards when these two were conversing together in subdued whispers, the knight silently admiring her grace and the maiden scarcely able to restrain her feelings, the thoughts which he longed to tell her, flamed in his heart. The same evening in the banqueting hall, when the music was sounding within its walls, he was Guta's inseparable companion, and eloquent words flowed from his lips telling her of the love which his eyes betrayed.

The proud stranger begged Guta for her love and swore to be hers; he told her he must at once return to his country where urgent duty called him, but that he would come back to claim her in three months' time. Then he would publicly sue for her hand and declare his name, which circumstances compelled him to keep secret for the time being.

Love will make any sacrifice; Guta accepted her lover's pledge willingly, and thus they parted under the assurance that they would soon meet again.

Five months had passed. That terrible time ensued when Germany became the battlefield of the party-struggles over the election of the emperor. Conrad IV. the last of the house of Hohenstaufen, had died in Italy. In the northern countries there was a great rising against William of Holland who was struggling for the

imperial throne; Alphonso of Castile was chosen king in one part of the country, while Richard of Cornwall, son of John, king of England, was elected in another; but Richard, having received most influential votes, was crowned at Aix-la-Chapelle, and from thence he started on a journey through the Rhine provinces, to the favour of which he had been chiefly indebted for his election.

*

Spring was casting her bright beams over waves and mountains in the valley of the Rhine, but in Falkenstein castle no ray of sunshine penetrated the gloom. Guta, pale and unhappy, sat within its walls, weaving dreams which seemed destined never to be fulfilled. Sometimes she saw her lover dying on a terrible battle field with her name on his lips, then again laughing and bright with a maiden from that far-off island in his arms, talking derisively of his sweetheart on the Rhine. She became more and more conscious that she had given him her first love, and that he had cruelly deceived her. Sorrow and grief had taken possession of her, and all her brother's efforts to amuse her and to distract her attention were in vain.

A great sound of trumpets was heard one day on the highway, and a troop of knights stopped at the castle. Guta saw the train of warriors from her window, where she had been sitting weeping. The count w. chivalrous hospitality received them, and led them into the banqueting-hall. His astonishment was great, when he recognised the bold Briton, the victor at the tournament in Cologne, as leader of this brilliant retinue, he who had broken his secret pledge to his beloved sister. A dark glance took the place of the friendly expression on his face. The Briton seemed to notice it and pressing Philip's hand said cordially, "I am Richard of Cornwall, elected Emperor of Germany, and I have come here to solicit the hand of your sister Guta, who promised herself to me five months ago in Cologne. I come late to redeem my promise, but my love is unchanged. I beg you to announce my arrival to her without betraying my name."

Philip bowed deeply before the illustrious guest, and the retainers respectfully retired to a distance. The great guest strode up and down the room impatiently. Then the doors were suddenly thrown open, and a beautiful figure appeared on the threshold, her face glowing with emotion.

With a low cry Guta threw herself into her lover's arms, and the first moments of their reunion were passed in silent happiness.

Philip now entered the room unperceived, and revealed the secret to his sister. The maiden in great confusion and shame stole a look at her lover's eyes, and he, drawing her gently to him, asked her to share all — even his throne with him.

Shortly afterwards Richard celebrated his marriage with imperial magnificence at the castle on the Rhine, which Philip thence forward called Gutenfels, in honour of his sister.

St. Goar

Loreley

Above Coblentz where the Rhine flows through hills covered with vineyards, there is a steep rock, round which many a legend has been woven — the Lurlei Rock. The boatman gazes up at its gigantic summit with awful reverence when his boat glides over the waters at twilight. Like chattering children the restless waves whisper round the rock, telling wonderful tales of its doings. Above on its gray head, the legend relates that a beautiful but false nymph, clothed in white with a wreath of stars in her flowing hair, used to sit and sing sweet songs, until a sad tragedy drove her forever away.

Long long ago, when night in her dark garment descended from the hills, and her silent comrade, the pale moon, cast a silver bridge over the deep green stream the soft voice of a woman was heard from the rock, and a creature of divine beauty was seen on its summit. Her golden locks flowed like a queenly mantle from her graceful shoulders, covering her snowwhite raiment so that her tenderlyformed body appeared like a cloud of light. Woe to the boatman who passed the rock at the close of day! As of old, men were fascinated by the heavenly song of the Grecian hero, so was the unhappy voyager allured by this being to sweet forgetfulness, his eyes, even as his soul, would be dazzled, and he could no longer steer clear of reefs and cliffs, and this beautiful siren only drew him to an early grave. Forgetting all else, he would steer towards her, already dreaming of having reached her; but the jealous waves would wash round his boat and at last dash him treacherously against the rocks. The roaring waters of the Rhine would drown the cries of agony of the victim who would never be seen again.

But the virgin to whom no one had ever approached, continued every night to sing soft and low, till darkness vanished in the first rays of light, and the great star of day drove the gray mists from the valley.

II.

Ronald was a proud youth and the boldest warrior at the court of his father, the Palatinate Count. He heard of this divine, enchanting creature, and his heart burned with the desire to behold her. Before having seen the water-nymph, he felt drawn to her by an irresistible power.

Under pretence of hunting, he left the court, and succeeded in getting an old sailor to row

him to the rock. Twilight was brooding over
the valley of the Rhine when the boat
approached the gigantic cliff; the departing sun
had long sunk below the mountains, and now
night was creeping on in silence; the evening
star was twinkling in the deep blue firmament.
Was it his protecting-angel who had placed it
there as a warning to the deluded young man?

He gazed at it in rapture for some time, until
a low cry from the old man at his side interrupted him. ”The Lorelei!“ whispered he, start-
led, ”do you see her — the enchantress?“ The
only answer was o soft murmur which escaped
from the youth. With wide-open eyes he looked
up and lo! there she was. Yes, this was she, this
wonderful creature! A glorious picture in a dark
frame. Yes, that was her golden hair, and those
were her flowing white garments.

She was hovering up above on the rocks
combing her beautiful hair; rays of light
surrounded her graceful head, revealing her
charms in spite of the night and the distance,
and as he gazed, her lips opened, and a song
thrilled through the silence, soft and plaintive
like the sweet notes of a nightingale on a still
summer evening.

From her height she looked down into the
hazy distance and cast at the youth a rapturous

look which sank down into his soul, thrilling his whole frame.

His eyes were fixed on the features of this celestial being where he read the sweet story of love . . . Rocks, stream, glorious night, all melted into a mist before his eyes, he saw nothing but the figure above, nothing but her radiant eyes. The boat crept along, too slowly for him, he could no longer remain in it, and if his ear did not deceive him, this creature seemed to whisper his name with unutterable sweetness, and calling to her, he dashed into the water.

A death-like cry echoed from the rocks . . . and the waves sighed and washed over the unhappy youth's corpse.

The old boatman moaned and crossed himself, and as he did so, lightning tore the clouds asunder, and a loud peal of thunder was heard over the mountains. Then the waves whispered gently below, and again from the heights above, sad and dying away, sounded the Lurlei's song.

III.

The sad news was soon brought to the Palatinate Count, who was overpowered with grief and anger. He ordered the false enchantress to be delivered up to him, dead or alive.

The next day a boat sailed down the Rhine, manned by four hardy bold warriors. The leader looked up sternly at the great rocks which seemed to be smilling silently down at him. He had asked permission to dash the diabolical seducer from the top of the rocks into the foaming whirlpool below, where she would find a certain death, and the count had readily agreed to this plan of revenge.

IV.

The first shades of twilight were gliding softly over mountain and hill.

The rock was surrounded by armed men, and the leader, followed by some daring comrades, was climbing up the side of the mountain the top of which was veiled in a golden mist, which the men thought were the last rays of sunset. It was a bright gleam of light enshrouding the nymph who appeared on the rocks, dreamingly combing her golden hair. She then took a string of pearls from her bosom, and with her slender white hand bound them round her forehead. She cast a mocking glance at the threadening men approaching her.

"What are the weak sons of the earth seeking up here on the heights?" said she, moving her rosy lips scornfully. "You sorceress!" cried the leader enraged, adding with a contemtuous smile, "You! We shall dash you down into the river below!"

An echoing laugh was heard over the mountain.

"Oh! the Rhine will come himself to fetch me!" cried the maiden.

Then bending her slender body over the precipice yawning below, she tore the jewels from her forehead, hurling them triumphantly into the waters, while in a low sweet voice she sang: —

"Haste thee, haste thee oh father dear!
Send forth thy steeds from the waters clear.
I will ride with the waves and the wind!"

Then a storm burst forth, the Rhine rose, covering its banks with foam. Two gigantic billows like snow-white steeds rose out of the depths, and carried the nymph down into the rushing current.

V.

The terrified messengers returned to the count, bringing him the tidings of this wonderful event.

Ronald, whose body a chance wave had washed up on the banks of the river, was deeply mourned throughout the country.

From this time forth, the Lorelei was never seen again. Only when night sheds her dark shadow on the hills, and the pale moon weaves

a silver bridge over the deep green stream, then the voice of a woman, soft and low, is heard echoing from the weird heights of the rocks.

The Lorelei has vanished, but her charm still remains.

Thou canst find it, O Wanderer, in the eyes of the maidens near the Rhine. It blooms on their cheeks, it lingers on their rosy lips, there thou wilt find its traces.

Arm thy heart, steel thy will, blindfold thine eye!

As a poet of the Rhine once wisely and warningly sang, "My son, my son, beware of the Rhine . . ."

The Lorelei has vanished, but her charm still remains.

Sterrenberg and Liebenstein

The Brothers

I.

In the middle ages, an old knight belonging to the court of the Emperor Conrad II. lived in a castle called Sterrenberg, near Boppard. The old warrior had two sons left to him. His wife had died many years before, and since her death, merry laughter had seldom been heard in the halls of the beautiful castle.

Soon a ray of sunshine seemed to break into these solemn rooms; a distant cousin at Rüdesheim had died, leaving his only child, a beautiful young girl, to the care of his relative.

The golden-haired Angela became the pet of the castle, and won the affection and friendship of the two sons by her engaging ways. What hat already happened hundred of times now happened among these young people, love replaced the friendship of the two young knights, and both tried to win the maiden's favour.

The old master of the castle noticed this change, and his father's heart forebode trouble.

Both sons were equally dear to him, but perhaps his first born, who had inherited his mother's gentle character, fulfilled his heart's desire more than the fiery spirit of Conrad the younger.

From the first moment when the orphan appeared at his family seat, he had conceived the thought that his favourite son Henry, who was heir to his name and estates would marry the maiden.

Henry loved Angela with a profound, sincere feeling which he seldom expressed.

His brother, on the contrary, made no secret of his ardent love, and soon the old man perceived with sorrow that the beautiful girl returned his younger son's passionate love. Henry, too, was not unaware of the happiness of this pair, and in generous self-denial he tried to bury his grief, and to rejoice heartily in his brother's success.

The distress of the elder brother did not escape Angela. She was much moved when she first remarked that his voice trembled on pronouncing her name, but soon love dazzled her eyes, so that the clouds on his troubled countenance passed unnoticed by her.

About this time St. Bernhard of Clairvaux came from France to the Rhine, preaching a second crusade against the Infidels. The fiery words of the saintly monk roused many

thousands to action; his appeal likewise reached the Castle of Sterrenberg.

Henry, though not envying his brother's happiness, felt that it would be impossible for him to be a constant vitness of it, and thus he was glad to answer this call, and to take up the cross.

Conrad, too, longing for action and dominated by the impulse of the moment, was stirred up by the witching charms which a crusade to Palestine offered. His adventurous soul, cramped up in this castle so far removed from the world, thirsted for the adventures, which he imagined were awaiting the crusaders in the far off East. In vain the tears and prayers of the young girl were shed, in vain was the sorrow of his father who begged him not do desert him.

The old man was in despair about the unbending resolutions of his sons.

"Who will remain at the castle of my fore-fathers, if you both abandon it now, perhaps never to return," cried he sorrowfully. "I implore you, my eldest son, you, the very image of your mother, to have pity on your father's gray hairs. And you, Conrad, have pity on the tears of your betrothed." The brothers remained silent. Then the eldest grasped the old man's hand, saying gently.

"I shall not leave you, my father."

"And you, Angela," said the younger to the weeping maiden, "you will try and bear this separation, and will plant a sprig of laurel to make a wreath for me when I return."

II.

The next day the young knight left the home of his forefathers. At first the maiden seemed inconsolable in her grief. But soon her love began to slumber like a tired child; on awakening from this drowsiness indignation seized her, whispering complainingly in her ear, and disturbing all the sweet memories in which the picture of her light-hearted lover gleamed forth, he who had parted from her for the sake of empty glory.

Now left to herself, she began to consider the proud youth who was forced to live under the same roof with his rejected love. She admired his good qualities which all seemed to have escaped her before, his great daring at the chase, his skill with weapons, and his many kind acts of pure friendship to her, with the view of sweetening the bitter separation from which she was suffering.

He seemed afraid of rousing the love which was still sleeping in his heart.

In the meantime Angela felt herself drawn more and more towards the knight; she wished to try and make him understand that her love for his younger brother had only been a youthful passion, which seemed to have flown when he left her. She felt unhappy when she understood that Henry, whom she now began really to love, seemed to feel nothing but brotherly affection for her, and she longed in her inmost soul for a word of love from him.

Henry was not unaware of this change in her affections, but he proudly smothered every rising thought in his heart for his brother's betrothed.

The old knight was greatly pleased when, one day, Angela came to him, and with tears in her eyes disclosed to him the secret of her heart.

He prayed God fervently to bring these two loving hearts together whom he believed were destined for one another by will of God. In his dreams he already saw Angela in her castle like his dead wife and his first-born son, rocking her little baby, a blue-eyed, fair-haired child. Then he would suddenly recollect his impetuous younger son fighting in the crusades, and his dreams would be hastily interrupted.

Just opposite to his ancestral hall he caused a proud fort to be built, and called it "Liebenstein", intending it for his second son when he returned from the Holy Land. The castle was hardly finished, when the old man died.

The crusade at last was at an end. All the knights from the Rhine country brought back the news with them on their return from the Holy Land, that Conrad had married a beautiful Grecian woman in the East, and was now on his way home with her.

Henry was beside himself with wrath on hearing this news. Such dishonourable conduct and shameful neglect seemed impossible to him, and going to the maiden he informed her of his brother's approaching return.

She turned very pale, her lips moved, but her tongue found no words.

III.

A large ship was seen one day sailing along the Rhine with strange flags waving on its masts. Angela saw it from her tower where she now spent many a long day reflecting on her unfortunate destiny, and she hastily called up the elder brother.

The ship approached nearer and nearer. Soon the cries of the boatmen could be heard, and the faces of the crew could be distinguished.

Suddenly the maiden uttered a cry, and threw herself weeping into the arms of the knight. The latter gazed a the vessel, his brows contracted. Yes! there on board, in shining armour, stood his brother, with a beautiful **strange** woman clinging to his arm.

The ship touched land. One of the first, Conrad sprang on shore. The two watchers in the tower disappeared. A man approached Conrad and informed him that the new castle was destined for him. The same day the impetuous knight sent notice of his arrival to Sterrenberg castle, but his brother answered him, that he would wait for him on the bridge, but would only meet sword in hand the faithless lover who had deserted his betrothed.

Twilight was creeping over the two castles. On the narrow ground separating the forts the brothers strove together in a deadly fight.

They were equally courageous, equally strong those two opponents, and their swords crossed swiftly, one in righteous anger, the other in wounded pride. But soon the elder received a blow, and the blood began to drop on his breastplate.

The bushes were at this moment suddenly pushed asunder, and a maiden, veiled in white, dashed in between the fighters thrusting them from each other. It was Angela, who cried out in a despairing voice:

"In God's name stop! and for your father's sake cease, ere it be too late. She for whom you have drawn your swords, is now going to take

the veil, and will beg God day and night to forgive you, Conrad, for your falseness, and will pray Him to bless you and your brother for ever."

Both brothers threw down their arms. Conrad, his head deeply bowed, covered his face with his hand. He did not dare to look at the maiden who stood there, a silent reproach to him. Henry took the weeping girl's hand.

"Come sister," said he, "such faithlessness does not deserve your tears."

They disappeared among the trees. Silently Conrad stood gazing after them. A feeling which he had never known seemed to rise up in his heart, and, bending his head, he wept bitterly.

IV.

The cloister, Marienburg, lay in a valley at some distance from the castles, and there Angela found pace. A wall was soon built up between the two forts Sterrenberg and Liebenstein, a silent witness of the enmity between the two brothers.

Banquet followed banquet in the newly built castle, and the beautiful Grecian won great triumphs among the knights of the Rhine.

But sorrow seemed to have taken possession of Sterrenberg castle. Henry had not wished to move the maiden from her purpose, but from the time of her departure, his strength faded away. At the foot of the mountain he caused a cloister to be built, and a few months later he passed away from this world, just on the same day that the bells were tolling for Angela's death.

The lord of Liebenstein was not granted a lasting happiness with his beautiful wife. She fled with a knight who had long enjoyed the lavish hospitality at castle Liebenstein. Conrad, overcome by sorrow and disgrace, threw himself from a pinnacle of the castle into the depths below.

The strongholds then fell into the hands of Knight Brömser of Rüdesheim, and since that time have fallen into ruins. The church and cloister still remain in the valley, and are the scene of many a pilgrimage.

Andernach

Genovefa

I.

In all the Rhine provinces the virtuous spouse of Count Siegfried of the Palatinate was esteemed and venerated. The people called her St. Genovefa, which name indeed she was worthy of, as she suffered cruel trials and sorrows. Siegfried's castle stood near the old town of Andernach, just at the time when Charles Martel was reigning over the Franks.

Siegfried and his young wife lived in peaceful unity, till a cloud came over their happiness. The much-dreaded Arabs from Spain had forced their way into Gaul, and were now marching northwards, burning and destroying all on their course. The enemies of the cross must be repulsed, unless the west was to share the fate of Africa, which had been subdued by the Mohametans.

The war-cry reached the Palatinate, and Siegfried had to go forth to the fight. Equipped in his armour, and having kissed his weeping wife, he bade farewell to the castle of his fathers. But he was sad at heart at leaving the spot where the happiest days of his life had been spent. He entrusted the administration of his property to Golo, his steward, and recommended his beloved wife very earnestly to his protection, begging her in turn to trust him in everything.

The poor countess was heart-broken at this bitter separation. She felt the loneliness of the castle deeply, she longed for his happy presence and the sound of his voice. She could never speak to Golo as to the friend to whose care her husband had recommended her. Her pure eyes shrank from the passionate look which gleamed in his. It seemed to her that he followed her every movement with a look which her childlike soul did not understand.

She missed her husband's presence more and more. She would go out on the balcony and weave golden dreams, and while she sat there, looking out over the hazy blue distance, she longed for the moment when Siegfried would return, when she could lean her head upon his breast, and tell him of the great happiness in store for them.

Perhaps the war against the heathens might last so long that she would be able to hold the pledge of their love joyfully out to him from the balcony on his return. And the countess' lovely face would be lit up with a gleam of blissful happiness, and she would while away the time on her favourite spot, dreaming and looking out into the hazy blue distance.

The secret aversion which the countess felt towards the steward was not without a reason. Her angel-like beauty had awakened lustful passion in Golo's breast, which he did not strive to hide. On the contrary his frequent intercourse with her, who was as gracious to him as to all her other inferiors, stirred his passion still more, and one day, losing all control, he threw himself at the countess' feet, declaring his love for her, and imploring her to return it. Genovefa was horrified at this confession. With indignation and scorn she rejected his love, forbidding him to appear before her as he had utterly forgotten his duty, and at the same time, threatening to complain of him to her husband. Golo's eyes flared up, and a deadly look of hatred gleamed from them.

He could hope for no pardon from his angry mistress. Besides, his pride would not allow him to seek it, and now his one desire was revenge. It only remained for him to follow his dastardly plan and to avoid Siegfried's wrath.

Hatred raged in his breast. He dismissed all the servants of the castle and put new ones of his own creation in their places. Then one day he appeared before the horrified countess, and openly accused her of being unfaithful to her husband far away.

Shame and wrath robbed Genovefa of speech. Golo explained to the servants who were standing around in silent amazement, that he had already informed the count of his wife's faithless conduct, and that he, Golo, as present administrator of the castle, now condemned the countess to be imprisoned in the dungeon.

The unhappy Genovefa awakened to find herself in an underground cell of the castle. She covered her face in deep sorrow, imploring Him who had sent her this trial, to help her in her present affliction. There after some time a son was born to her. She baptized him with her tears, giving him the name of Tristan, which means "full of sorrows".

II.

Siegfried had already been absent six months. He had fought like a hero in many a desperate battle. The fanatical followers of Mohamet having crossed the Pyrenees, struggled with wild enthusiasm, hoping to subdue the rest of western Europe to the doctrines of Islam by fire and sword. In several encounters, the Franks had been obliged to give way to their power. These unbridled hordes had already penetrated into the heart of Gaul, when Charles first appeared and engaged the Arabs in the bloody battle of Tours. From morning till evening the struggle on which hung the fate of Europe raged. And there Charles proved himself worthy of the name of Martel "the hammer", which he afterwards received.

Siegfried fought at the leader's side like a lion; but towards evening a Saracen's lance pierced him, and though the wound was not mortal, yet he was obliged to remain inactive for several months on a sick-bed, where he thought with longing in his heart of his loving wife by the Rhine.

A messenger arrived one day at the camp bearing a parchment from Golo, Siegfried's steward. The count gazed long at the fateful letter, trying to comprehend its meaning. What he had read, ran thus: "Your wife is unfaithful to you and has betrayed you for the sake of Drago, a servant, who ran away." The hero crushed the letter furiously in his hand, a groan escaping from his white lips. Then he started off accompanied by a few followers, and rode towards the Ardennes, never stopping till he reached his own fort. A man stood on the balcony, looking searchingly out into the distance, and seeing a cloud of dust approaching in which a group of horsemen soon became visible, his eyes gleamed triumphantly.

A stately knight advanced, his charger stamping threateningly on the drawbridge. Golo, with hypocritical emotion stood before the count, who had now alighted from his foaming horse, and informed him again of what had happened. "Where is the evil-doer who has stained the honour of my house, where is he, that I may crush his life out?" cried Siegfried in a fury.

"My lord, I have punished the wretch deservedly and lashed him out of the castle," answered Golo in a stern voice, sighing deeply.

The count made a sign to Golo whose false eyes gleamed with devilish joy, to lead the way.

Siegfried entered the dungeon, followed by his servants and also by those who had travelled with him. Genovefa listened breathlessly in her prison, with a loved name trembling on her lips and a prayer to God in her heart. Now the terrible trial would come to an end, now she would leave this dungeon of disgrace triumphantly, and exchange the crown of thorns for the victor's wreath.

The bolt was unfastened, firm steps and men's voices were heard, the iron doors were dashed open. She snatched her slumbering child, the pledge of their love, and held it towards her dear husband. His name was on her lips, but before she could utter it, a cry of agony escaped her. He had cast her from him and, his accusations falling like blows from a hammer on her head, the poor innocent countess fell senseless to the ground. The next day two servants lead mother and child out into the forest, where with their own hands, they were to kill her who had been so unfaithful to her husband, and her child also. They were to bring back two tongues to the count as a proof that they had obeyed his orders.

The servants drove them into the wildest depths of the forest where only the screams of birds of prey broke the silence. They drew their knives. But the poor countess fell on her knees, and holding up her little child, implored them to spare their lives, if not for her sake, at least for the sake of the helpless child. Pity entered the two men's hearts and withheld their hands. Dragging the mother and child still deeper into the forest, they turned away hastily, leaving their victims to themselves.

They brought two harts' tongues to the count, informing him that they had fulfilled his orders.

III.

Genovefa's tired feet wandered through the unknown forest, her child crying with hunger. She prayed fervently to Heaven in her despair, and tears were sent to relieve the dull pain in her heart, after which she felt more composed, and her child was soon sweetly slumbering. To her great astonishment she perceived a cavern near her, where she could take shelter, and as if God wished to show that He had heard her prayer, a white doe came towards the cavern, rubbing herself caressingly against the abandoned woman. Willingly the gentle animal allowed the little child to be suckled. The next day the doe came back again, and Genovefa thanked God from the depths of her heart. She found roots, berries, and plants, to support herself, and every day the tame doe came back to her, and at last remained always with her.

Days, weeks, and months passed. Her unfaltering faith had rendered her agony less. In time she learned to forgive her husband who had condemned her unjustly, and she even pardoned him who had taken such bitter revenge on her. Her lovely cheeks had become thinner, but the forest winds had breathed a soft red into them, and the child who had no cares nor gnawing pain in its heart, grew into a beautiful little boy.

IV.

At the castle on the Rhine, sorrow was a constant guest since this terrible event had happened. Siegfried's burning anger had sunk into sorrow, and often when he was wandering restlessly through the rooms so rich in sweet memories, where now a deserted stillness reigned, the agony awoke again in his heart. He now repented of his hastiness, and a voice whispered in his ear that he had been too severe in his cruel punishment, that he had condemned too quickly, and that he should have considered what he could have done to mitigate her punishment.

When these haunting voices pursued him, he would hurry away from the castle and its loneliness, not being able to bear the torment of his thoughts. Then to forget his trouble, he would follow the chase with the yelping hounds. But he only seldom succeeded in dulling his misery. Everywhere he seemed to see the pale face of a woman looking imploringly at him.

The state of his master's soul had not escaped Golo, and this crafty man cringed the more to the sorrowful count, feigning to care for his welfare. A starving person accepts even the bread which a beggarman offers, and Siegfried, supposing his steward wished to compensate him for his loss, accepted willingly every proof

of devotion, and recompensed him with his favour, at the same time hating the man in his inmost soul who had rendered him such a terrible service.

One day the count rode out to the chase, accompanied by only a few retainers, one of whom was Golo. Siegfried pressed deeper than was his custom into the forest. A milkwhite doe sprang up before him and sportsmanlike, he chased this singular animal through the bushes, hoping to shoot it. His spear had just grazed it, when it disappeared suddenly into a cavern. A woman whose ragged garments scarcely covered her nakedness, leading a little boy by the hand, suddenly came out of the opening in the rock, and the doe, seeking protection, rubbed herself against her. She looked at the hunter, but her limbs trembled so that she could scarcely stand, only her large sad eyes gazed wistfully at him. A stifled cry, half triumphant, half a groan, escaped from her lips and she threw herself at the count's feet. From the voice which for long months had only moved in earnest prayer or in low sweet words to the child, now flowed solemn protestations of her innocence. Her words burned like fire into the soul of the count, and drawing her to his breast, he kissed her tears, and then sank at her feet imploring her pardon.

He pressed his little boy to his heart, overcome with gratitude and happiness, and wept with joy, calling him by a thousand affectionate names.

Then at the sound of his bugle-horn his retinue hastened towards him, Golo among them.

"Do you know these two?" thundered out the count to the latter, tearing him from the throng and conducting him to Genovefa.

The wretch, as if struck by a club, broke down and, clasping his master's knees, he confessed his wickedness and begged for mercy. Siegfried thrust him contemptuously from him, refusing sternly, in spite of the countess' intercession, to pardon his crime. Golo was bound and led away, and a disgraceful death was his reward.

Now began a time of great happiness for Siegfried and his saint-like wife, and they lived in undisturbed peace with their little son.

In gratitude to Heaven Siegfried caused a church to be built on the spot where the white doe had appeared to him first. The countess often made a pilgrimage to this house of God, to thank Him who had caused her tears to be turned into joy. Then a day came when her corpse was carried into the forest, and was buried in the church. Even now in Laach, the wanderer is shown the church and the tombstone, also the cavern where she suffered so much. Thus the name of St. Genovefa will last to all time.

The Drachenfels

When the wanderer has left the "city of the Muses", Bonn, he perceives to the left the mighty summits of the Seven Mountains. The rocky point of one of these hills is still crowned by the tower and walls of an old knight's castle. A most touching legend is related of the mountain with the terrible name.

In the first centuries after the birth of the world's Redeemer, the Germans on the left side of the Rhine accepted willingly the doctrines of the cross; Maternus, a disciple of the great Apostle, had brought them over from Gaul. At first the pious messenger of Christ worked among the heathen tribes in vain. They persisted in their paganism, and even prevented the priests from coming into their country.

At that time there was a terrible dragon living in the hollow of the rock which even now is called the Dragon's hole. He was of a hideous form, and every day he used to leave his den and rage through the forests and valleys, threatening men and animals. Human strength was powerless against this monster; the people thought that an angry deity had his abode in this terrible beast, so they bestowed godlike honours on him, sacrificing criminals and prisoners to him.

A tribe of heathens lived at the foot of the mountain. These men, desirous of war, often made raids on the neighbouring countries, carrying fire and sword among their Christian brothers They once crossed the water, plundering the land and making prisoners of the people. Among the latter there was one most lovely maiden, whose beauty and grace inflamed two of the leaders so much, that each of them desired to have her for himself. One was called Horsrik the Elder, a famous chieftain, known to have the strength of a bear and the wildness of a tiger; the other, Rinbold, of a less rough nature, but of equal bravery.

The beautiful maiden turned aside shuddering when she saw the two chief's glaring eyes. contending for possession of her. All round were their men intoxicated with victory. The struggle for the Christian maid affected the two leaders more than the division of the booty. Soon the angry words of the two opponents found an echo in the hearts of the men standing round.

Horsrik, the much-feared fighter, claimed her, and was received with cheers. Rinboldt, the proud young chieftain, claimed her also, — great applause greeted him. The former glared sternly, grasping his club in a threatening manner. The highpriest, an old man with silver-white hair and stern features, stepped in between the two combatants, and in a voice surging with anger he said:

"Cursed be every dissension for the possession of this stranger! A Christian must not disunite the noblest of our tribe. A daughter of those we hate, she shall fall to nobody's share. She, the author of so much strife, shall be sacrificed to the Dragon, and shall be dedicated to Woden's honour at the next rising of the sun."

The men murmured applause, Horsrik more than the rest. The maiden held her head upright. Rinbold, the proud young chieftain, looked sorrowfully at her angellike face.

II.

Early the following day before the sun had poured his bright beams on the earth, the valley showed signs of life. Through the dusk of the forest a noisy procession moved upwards towards the highest point, the priest in the middle, behind him the prisoner, pale but resolute. Silently, for her Lord's sake, she had allowed the priest to bind her forehead as a victim, and to place consecrated flowers in her loose flowing hair. Many a sympathetic look from the crowd had been cast at the steadfast maiden. The young chieftain was stricken with pain at the sight of her death-like countenance.

There stood the projecting rock which had often been dishonoured by human blood. The fanatical priests wound ropes round the maiden's body, and then tied her to St. Woden's tree which overhung the precipice. No complaint escaped the Christian's white lips, no tears glistened in her eyes which were glancing up at the morning sky. The throng of people moved off, waiting silently in the distance to see what would happen.

The first rays of the sun streamed over the mountain; they lighted up the wreath of flowers in the maiden's hair, playing about her lovely face, and crowning it with glory. The Christian maid was awaiting death, as a bride awaits her bridegroom, her lips moving slightly as in prayer.

A gloomy sound came up from the depths. The Dragon started from his den, spitting fire on his path. He cast a look at his victim there on the spot which his blood-thirsty maw knew so well. He raised his scaly body, thus letting his sharp claws be more visible, moved his snaky tail in a circle, and showed his gaping mouth. Snorting the monster crawled along, shooting flames out of his bloodshot eyes.

A shudder of death crept over the maiden at the sight of this awful beast. Tremblingly she tore a sparkling golden crucifix from her breast,

held it towards the monster piteously, and called on her Lord in a heart-rending voice. Wonder of wonders! Raising himself, as if struck by lightning, the monster turned, dashing himself backwards over the jagged stones into the waters below, and disappearing in the river among the falling rocks.

Wondering cries arose from the waiting heathens. Astonishment and wonder were depicted on every face. In quiet submission, her eyes half-closed, the maiden stood, praying to Him who had saved her. The cords fell from her sides; two strong arms caught her and carried her into the midst of the astonished crowd. She raised her eyes and perceived the younger of the two chieftains. His rough warlike hand had seized hers. The young man bent his knees as if to a heavenly being, and touched her white fingers with his lips, loud applause greeted him on all sides.

The old priest came forward, the people waiting in great expectation. "Who had saved her from certain destruction? Who was the God who so visibly aided His own?" asked he solemnly of the Christian. With bright eyes the maiden answered triumphantly:

"This picture of Christ has crushed the Dragon and saved me. The salvation of the world and the welfare of man lies in Him." The priest glanced at the crucifix with reverent awe.

"May it soon lighten your spirit and those of all these people round," said the maiden earnestly. "It will reveal greater wonders than this to you, for our God is great."

The maiden and all the other prisoners were conducted back to their own country. But the former soon returned again, accompanied by a Christian priest. The voice of truth and innocence worked wonders in the hearts of the heathens. Thousands were converted and baptized. The old priest and Rinbold were the first who bowed their heads in submission to the new doctrine. Great rejoicings were held among the tribe when the maiden gave her hand to the young chieftain. A Christian temple was erected in the valley, and a splendid castle was built on the summit of the rocks for the newly-married couple. For about ten centuries their descendants flourished there, a very powerful race in the Rhine countries.

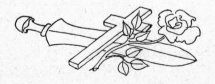

The Monk of Heisterbach

In olden times in a lovely valley near the Seven Mountains, stood a cloister called Heisterbach. Even now parts of the walls of this old monastery remain, and it was not by the hand of time, but by the barbarism of foolish warfare, that its halls fell into ruins. The monks were driven away, the abbey was pulled down, and the stones were used for the building of a fortress.

Since that time, so the country folk relate, the spirits of the banished monks wander nightly among the ruins, raising mute accusations against their persecutors and the destroyers of their cells. Among them there was one, Gebhard, the last Prior of Heisterbach, who now, they say, wanders about the graves of the monks, and also haunts the burial-places of the Masters of Löwenburg and Drachenburg.

In the Middle Ages the monks of Heisterbach were very famous. Many a rare copy of the Holy Scriptures, many highly learned piece of writing was sent out into the world from this hermitage, telling of the industry and learning of the pious monks.

There was one brother, still young in years, who distinguished himself by his learning. He was looked up to by all the other brethren, and even the gray-haired Father Prior had recourse to his stores of knowledge. But the poisonous worm of doubt began to gnaw at his soul; the mirror of his faith was blurred by his deep meditations. His keen eye would often wander over the faded parchment on which the living word of God was written while his childlike believing heart, humbly submitting itself, would lamentingly cry out, "Lord, I believe, help Thou mine unbelief!" Like a ghost his restless doubts would hover about him, making his soul the scene of tormenting struggle.

One night with flushed face he had been meditating over a parchment. At daybreak he still remained engrossed in his thoughts. The morning sun threw his bright rays over the heavens, casting playful beams on the written roll in the monk's hands.

But he saw them not, his thoughts were wholly taken up by a passage which for months past had ever been hidden to him and had been the constant subject of his reflections, "A thousand years are but as a day in Thy sight."

His brain had already long tormented itself over the obscure words of the Psalmist, and with a great effort he had striven to blot it out of his memory, and now the words danced again before his weary eyes, growing larger and larger. Those confusing black signs seemed to become a sneering doubt hovering round him: "A thousand years are but as a day in Thy sight."

He tore himself away from the silent cell, seeking the cool solitude of the cloister-gardens. There with a heavy heart he paced the paths, torturing himself with horrid doubts.

His eyes were fixed on the ground, his mind was far away from the peaceful garden, and without being aware of what he was doing, he left the cloister gardens and wandered out into the neighbouring forest. The birds in the trees greeted him cordially, the flowers opened their eyes at his approach; but the wretched man heard and saw nothing but the words: "A thousand years are but as a day in Thy sight."

His wandering steps grew feeble, his feverish brain weary from want of sleep. Then the monk sank down on a stone, and laid his troubled head against a tree.

A sweet, peaceful dream stole over his spirit. He found himself in spheres glowing with light; the waters of Eternity were rushing round the throne of the Most High; creation appeared and praised His works, and Heaven extolled their glory; from the worm in the dust, which no earthly being has been able to create, to the eagle soaring above the heights of the earth: from the grain of sand on the sea-shore, to the gigantic crater, which, at the Lord's command, vomits fire out of its throat which has been closed for thousands of years: they all spoke with one voice which is not heard by the haughty, being only manifest and comprehensible to the humble. These were the words of Him who created them, be it in six days or in six thousand years, "A thousand years are but as a day in Thy sight."

With a slight shudder the monk opened his eyes.

"I believe Lord! help Thou my unbelief," murmured he, taking heart.

The bell sounded in the distance. They were ringing for vespers; sunset was already gleaming through the forest.

The monk hastily turned towards the cloister. The chapel was lighted up, and through the half-opened door he could see the brothers in their stalls. He hurried noiselessly to his place, but to his astonishment he found that another monk was there; he touched him lightly on the shoulder, and strange to tell, the man he saw was unknown to him. The brothers, now one, now another, raised their heads and looked in silent questioning at the new comer.

A peculiar feeling seized the poor monk, who saw only strange faces round him. Growing pale, he waited till the singing was over.

Confused questions seemed to pass along the rows.

The Prior, a dignified old man with snow-white hair, approached.

"What is your name, strange brother?" asked he in a gentle, kind tone. The monk was filled with dismay. "Maurus", murmured he in a trembling voice. "St. Bernhard was the Abbot who received my vows, in the sixth year of the reign of King Conrad, whom they called the Frank."

Incredulous astonishment was depicted on the brothers' countenances.

The monk raised his face to the old Prior and confessed to him how he had wandered out in the early morning into the cloister-gardens, how he had fallen asleep in the forest, and had not wakened till the bell for vespers sounded.

The Prior made a sign to one of the brothers. Then turning to the monk he said: "It is almost three hundred years since the death of St. Bernhard and of Conrad, whom they called the Frank."

The cloister annals were brought, and it was there found that three hundred years had passed since the days of St. Bernhard. The Prior also read the following note.

"A doubter disappeared one day from the cloister, and no one ever knew what became of him."

A shudder ran through the monk's limbs. This was he, this brother Maurus who had now come back to the cloister after three hundred years! What the Prior had read sounded in his ears as if it were the trumpet of the Last Judgment. Three hundred years!

With wide-open eyes he gazed before him, then stretched forth his hands as if seeking for help. The brothers supported him, observing him at the same time with secret dismay; his face had become ashy pale, like that of a dying person, the narrow circle of hair on his head had become snow-white.

"My brothers," murmured he in a dying voice, "value the imperishable word of the Lord at all times, and never try to fathom what he in His wisdom has veiled from us. May my example never be blotted out of your memory. Only to-day the words of the Psalmist were revealed to me. "A thousand years are but as a day in Thy sight. May he have mercy on me, a poor sinner." He sank lifeless to the ground, and the brothers, greatly moved, repeated the prayers for the dead over his body.

Cologne

Richmodis of Aducht

It was about the middle of the fifteenth century.

The shadows of death hovered above the holy City of Cologne. A strange figure in dark garments huried with quick steps through the streets and lanes. It was the plague. Its poisonoos breath penetrated into cottages and palaces, extinguishing the lives of many thousands.

The grave diggers marked innumerable houses with a black cross, to warn the passersby that the destroying angel had entered there. The roll of the dead rose to such numbers that it was impossible to bury them all in the customary manner. Therefore the bodies of the unfortunate people were thrown together into a common grave, covered only scantily with earth and marked with a plain wooden cross.

Woe and sorrow thus filled the old City of Cologne.

On the New-market, close to the Church of the Apostles, in a splendid mansion, the rich Magistrate, Mengis of Aducht lived. Wealth could not save his house from the dreadful epidemic, his youthful and lovely wife, Rich-

modis, was seized with the plague and died.
The grief of her lord was boundless. He passed
the whole night by the remains of his beloved
spouse, dressed her himself in the white wed-
ding gown she had worn as a happy bride a
few years before, decorated the coffin with
sweet white flowers, and covered her with the
precious jewels and costly rings she had loved
so much. Then she was buried.

Night approached, and the clear starry sky
looked peacefully down on the afflicted town.

Perfect stillness prevailed in God's acre. —
Suddenly a jarring sound like the opening of
an old rusty lock was heard, and two dark
shadows glided among the graves, on and on
till they stopped before the fresh mould which
enclosed the body of Richmodis of Aducht. —
Those two knew the spot, and well they might,
for they were the grave-diggers, and had prepared this grave themselves on the previous
day.

They were present when the lid of the coffin
was screwed down, and had with hungry looks
coveted the glittering precious stones Richmodis
was to be buried with.

Now they had come to rob the dead body.
With spade and shovel the wreaths and flowers
were quickly removed from the mound, the
earth dug up and the coffin laid bare. In

feverish haste, spurred on by their greed, they burst the lid open, and the dim light of their lantern fell full on the mild pale face of the dead woman. With haste the bolder of the two wretches loosened the white waxen hands folded together as in prayer, and tried to tear off the rings.

Suddenly the body quivered, and the white hands spread out. Aghast the robbers dropped their tools, scrambled in utmost terror out of the grave, and fled as if chased by the furies.

A painful long sigh rose from the depth of the grave, and after some time the white form of Richmodis who had been buried alive, emerged from the tomb.

With wide open eyes, full of horror, she looked down into the ghastly bed she had just left. — Could it really be true, or was it only a frightful dream?

God's acre was silent, but for the rustling of the autumn leaves of the weeping willows Stillness of death everywhere! — No answer came to her faint cry for help — The horror of her situation however wakened her declining strength. She took up the lantern which the robbers had left behind them and with feeble steps reached the entrance of the churchyard.

The streets were desolate. The stars overhead alone perceived the slowly moving form, every now and then resting against the walls of the houses. — At last she reached the Newmarket and stood before the door of her home. Dark and quiet it seemed. But from the window in the magistrate's room a faint light shone forth. A quiver ran through the frame of the poor wife, and a wild longing desire seized her to be sheltered by his loving arms and to feel in his embrace that she had really returned to life again.

With a last effort she seized the knocker, and listened with newly awakened hope to the tapping sound which rang clear through the night.

A few minutes elapsed. Then an old servant peeping out of the window in the door, perceived the white ghostly figure of his late mistress. Horror seized him, his hair stood on end. Richmodis called him by his name and begged him to open the door. At the sound of her voice the old man started, ran upstairs, dashed into his master's room uttering incoherent sounds, and stammering: "O Lord, the dead rise; outside stands our good Mistress and demands entrance!" But the Magistrate shook his head in deep grief: "Richmodis, my beloved wife is dead and will never return, never, never," he repeated in unspeakable sorrow, "I will rather believe that my two white horses will burst from their halters in the stable and mount the theirs to the tower."

A terrible sound suddenly filled the quier house, a noise like thunder was heard, and Mengis of Aducht and his servant saw the two white steeds tearing and tramping in haste upstairs.

A moment later two horses looked out of the tower windows into the night, and shortly afterwards the Magistrate laughing and crying with joy at the same time, held in his arms his wife who had returned from the grave.

For many years Richmodis lived happily with her husband, surrounded by several lovely children. Deep piety remained the motive power of Richmodis' being, and nobody ever saw her smile again.

If you come to Cologne, reader, you will still see the old house of the Aduchts at the New-market, with two white wooden horses' heads looking out of the top window.

The Goblins

This story goes back to the "good old times" of which we modern people always speak with a sigh of regret.

It was then when good-natured goblins appeared to mortal eyes, and tried to render the life of the troubled human race a little more cheerful. In groves and dens they had magnificent dwellings and watched there over the enormous mineral treasures of the earth.

Often these beneficent elves were busy miners or sometimes clever artisans. We all know that they manufactured the precious trinkets and arms of the Nibelungen treasure.

Deep in the interior of the earth they lived happily together, ruled over by a king. They could be called the harmless friends of darkness, because they were not allowed to come into broad daylight. If they did so, they were transformed into stones.

The goblins did not always remain underground. On the contrary they often came to the earth's surface through certain holes, called goblin-holes, but they always avoided meeting man.

Alas! the advance of civilisation has driven these friendly spirits gradually from the places where they used to do so much good. None of us, I am sure has, ever had the good luck of meeting one of them.

The goblins were of different sizes. Sometimes they were as small as one's thumb, sometimes as large as the hand of a child of four years old. The most remarkable feature of these tiny figures was the enormous head and the pointed hump that so often adorned their backs. Their look was on the whole more comical than ugly. German people used to call them "Heinzchen" or "Heinzelmännchen".

A long time ago the good town of Cologne was inhabited by a host of dwarfs, and the honest population knew a great many stories about them. The workmen and artisans especially had, through the assistance of the little wights, far more holidays than are marked in the calendar.

When the carpenters for instance were lying on their benches in sweet repose, those little men came swiftly and stealthily along, they took up the tools and chiselled and sawed and hammered with a will, and thus, records the poetical chronicles which I am quoting, before the carpenters woke up, the house stood there finished.

In the same way things went on with the baker. While his lads were snoring, the little goblins came to help. They groaned under the load of heavy corn-sacks, they kneaded and weighed the flour, lifted and pushed the bread into the oven, and before the lazy bakers opened their eyes, the morning bread, brown and crisp, was lying in rows on the table.

The butchers, too, could speak of similar agreeable experiences. The good little men chopped, mixed and stirred with all their might, and when the drowsy butcher opened his eyes at last, he found the fresh, steaming sausages adorning the walls of his shop.

The cooper also enjoyed the help of the busy dwarfs, and even the tailor could not complain of the goblins having neglected him.

Once Mr. Cotton, a clever tailor, had the honour of making a Sunday coat for the mayor of the town. He worked diligently at it, but you can easily imagine that in the heat of the summer afternoon, the needle soon dropped from his hand, and he fell fast asleep. Hush! — look there. One little goblin after the other crept cautiously from his hiding place.

They climbed on the table and began the tailor's work and stitched and sewed and fitted and pressed, as if they had been masters of the needle all their lives.

When Master Cotton awoke, he found to his great joy the mayor's Sunday coat ready made,

and so neatly and well done that he could present the magnificent garment with pride to the head of the town.

The pretty wife of Mr. Cotton looked at this master-piece of her husband's art with a mischievous twinkle in her eyes.

In the night when her husband had fallen asleep, she rose from her bed without making the slightest noise, and scattered pease all over the floor of the workshop; she then put a half-finished suit on the table. She kept a small lantern hidden under her apron, and waited behind the door listening. Soon after the room was full of little men all tumbling, falling, and slipping over the pease. Yells and screams rose at the same time. The poor little men were indeed much bruised and hurt. Without stopping they ran downstairs and disappeared.

The tailor's wife heard the noise, and thought it good sport. When the yells were loudest, she suddenly opened the door to see her visitors, but she came too late. Not a single goblin was left behind.

Since that time the friendly dwarfs have never more been seen in Cologne, and in other places also they have entirely disappeared.

*

Xanten

Siegfried

Siegfried, — and as we pronounce this glorious name, the hero looks forth at us with shining eyes, for was not Siegfried the perfect embodiment of all that was beautiful and good?

For centuries stories have been told and poems have been sung of the bold adventures of the young hero, whose energy only found satisfaction in victorious fights.

The original name of the small town on the lower Rhine now called Xanten, was "Ad Santos", "peace for the saints". It was thus named on account of the pious warriors of the Theban legion who in the fourth century had boldly died there for their creed under their leader, Victor.

At the time to which our story refers, a mighty stronghold formed the centre of the little town Xanten. A king called Siegmund with his wife Siegelinde and their son Siegfried lived there.

While a mere boy, Siegfried had already a kingly stature, and an almost untamable disposition of mind. When he was only thirteen years of age, his longing for grand deeds was so great that he found it impossible to remain inactive at home. From old songs and legends which the minstrels recited in his father's castle, he had heard so much of bold adventures and brilliant exploits performed by his forefathers, that he was most anxious to follow in their steps. He felt strong and valiant enough to undertake like the heroes of old, dangerous journeys. Therefore young Siegfried left one day his ancestral halls, and wandered southwards along the clear blue river. He soon found an opportunity of testing his courage.

At the foot of the Seven Mountains lived a celebrated armourer called Mimer, renowned for making excellent swords. Our hero liked this warlike trade, and he asked the master to receive him as an apprentice, that he might learn the praiseworthy art of forging a good sword for himself. The armourer agreed, and Siegfried remained at Mimer's workshop. The journeymen with whom the youth had to work, soon learned the enormous strength of their new companion. The boy, often not knowing how to give expression to his desire for action, would take up his fellow-workmen, lift them high into the air, and drop them, not always softly to the ground. Or when his anger was roused, he would imprint black and blue marks on their backs with his strong fists. Once he even smashed with one stroke of his hammer all the

iron bars in the armoury, and knocked the anvil into the ground with a mighty blow.

Mimer looked on with dismay, amazed at the boy's almost supernatural strength, but fearing that Siegfried's wrath might some time turn against him, he thought to rid himself of his dangerous apprentice, and conceived a cunning plan to kill him. A horrible dragon lived in the neigbouring forest, which tore every wanderer to prieces who chanced to cross its way. Mimer ordered Siegfried to fetch a sack from the charcoal-burner in that forest, well knowing that the boy would never return thence.

The youth, without knowing the danger he was about to meet, went cheerfully on his way. In the middle of the thick wood he kindled a charcoal-kiln, and amused himself by putting big burning branches and young trees into the fire.

Suddenly the monster came swiftly creeping on its huge claws. Curving its shimmering body the ugly beast opened wide its jaws to devour the young charcoal-burner. Siegfried's eyes brightened up at the prospect of an encounter with the terrible animal before him. Without a moment's hesitation, he tore a flaming beam out of the kiln, and pushed its burning end deep into the open mouth of the dragon.

Roaring with pain the monster turned round beating violently with its prickly tail, trying in its agony to crush Siegfried. But he, jumping skilfully aside, rapidly dealt it heavy blows, and succeeded at last in smashing its head with a large piece of rock. He severed the head from the body, and threw it into the blazing flames. To his astonishment he observed how a stream of grease gushed from the burning pile, and collected in a pool at his feet.

Close by the charcoal-kiln stood an old lime-tree. A little bird sang merrily in its branches. Siegfried, involuntarily listening to the clear strain, made out the following words: "If you would be covered with horn, and become invulnerable, undress yourself and plunge into the pool".

Siegfried quickly threw his clothes off and anointed his whole body with the dragon's grease. While thus occupied a leaf from the old lime-tree above dropped between his shoulders. This part of the hero's body remained without horn. When he had finished, he took up the monster's head and returned to Mimer's workshop. The nearer he got to the smithy, the more his rage against his wicked master increased. Mimer had seen the boy from afar approaching with the trophy of his fight, and had hidden in great fear.

Siegfried however soon found him out and slew him on the spot. Then he forged a good two edged sword and shining armour for himself, and having saddled the best horse of Mimer's stable, he left the smithy to look for new adventures.

For a long time he travelled aimlessly about, saw mountains and valleys, rivers and lakes, cities and hamlets, until he at last arrived at the seashore. He embarked with his good horse, and was cast by a gale on the rocky coast of an unknown country. The noble animal climbed courageously up the stony beach, and carried its rider to an enchanted castle which was surrounded by a wall of flames. For a moment Siegfried stood irresolute. Suddenly the voice of the little bird sounded again above him, "Break the charm. Straight into the flames with a bold dash. A most lovely maiden will be thy reward".

The youth took courage, spurred his steed, and with a plunge horse and rider disappeared in the flames, which were at once extinguished. The charm was broken. Before him lay a wonderful castle. Siegfried penetrated into its interior, and was amazed to find every living creature in a profound sleep within; the horses in their stalls, the grooms in the stables, the cook at the hearth. When he entered the high hall a lovely scene presented itself to his view. On a couch the most exquisite form of a woman lay sleeping. Her golden hair was strewn with precious stones, and her limbs were clothed in the most costly garments.

The young hero looked for a while, lost in admiration. Then bending down to her, he pressed a passionate kiss on her rosy lips. Brunhilde, the fair sleeper, opened her eyes, and at the same time every living being in the castle awoke.

At the prospect of new adventures Siegfried could not be kept back a long time by Brunhilde. They parted with the solemn promise of meeting again.

The legend of Siegfried's youthful exploits and his home-coming is full of romance and happiness. But if we listen to the continuation of his story we shall find how every human feeling has its place in the hero's biography, great joy, deep sorrow, passionate love, glowing hatred, heroism and perfidy, cowardice and high courage, until at last the legend of Siegfried ends in a pitiful wail of grief.

Cleve

Lohengrin

The weathercock on the ancient stronghold at Cleves is a swan, and in olden times the dynasty that ruled over the lovely country round Cleves also had a swan in their crest. A legend, tragic and beautiful, preserved to posterity forever in Richard Wagner's lovely opera, is connected with it, — the legend of Lohengrin.

Long centuries ago deep sorrow brooded over the walls of the castle at Cleves. Its mistress, the Duchess Elsa was in great distress. Her beloved husband had died, and his remains had been brought to their last resting-place. As soon as the tomb had closed over them, one of the late Duke's vassals, Telramund, rose in revolt, and imperiously claimed the right to reign over the dukedom. The audacious man went so far as to ask the widowed Duchess to become his wife, declaring that this was the only means of saving her rank, which the death of her husband had deprived her of.

Elsa, the youthful and lovely mistress, implored the knights of her dominion to assist

116

her in her trouble, and to take up arms against the rebel. But Telramund, little disconcerted by this appeal, offered to fight in single combat with anybody who dared to take up the quarrel with him, well knowing that, on account of his immense strength, nobody would dare to become his adversary.

The days passed in deepest sorrow for the unfortunate Duchess. The moment was approaching when the rebel would make bold to proclaim openly his claims before the whole assembled nobility on the open space before the castle. The fatal hour came. Pale, her face covered by her widow's veil, her queenly form enveloped in mourning garments, Elsa descended from her castle to the assembly. The large plain was crowded with a throng of people, and glittered with the brilliant armour of the knights.

The unfaithful vassal, covered from head to foot in shining armour, came forward with bold steps and claimed in a loud voice the hand and dominion of the Duchess. The knights around, deluded by his valiant appearance and the firmness of his voice, broke into loud applause. Some of the crowd joined them in their cry of approbation, but most of the people looked on, full of pity and admiration for their youthful mistress.

No answer to his first challenge having come, Telramund repeated his audacious demand, offering again to fight in single combat anybody who dared to accept it. His eyes glanced defiantly over the brilliant multitude of knights. He perceived with triumphant joy, how they all shrank from fighting with him. — Elsa looked still paler than before.

For a third time the challenge of Telramund was heard. It sounded clearly over the whole plain. But none of the bright warriors came forward to take up the combat for Elsa's sake.

On the contrary deep silence followed the third challenge, and everybody's eyes were fixed on the forsaken princess who looked in her abandoned position still more lovely. The little hope that had till that moment given her strength to bear her misfortune, had now entirely vanished. In her utter desolation she offered a fervent prayer to heaven. On her rosary, so the legend records, a little silver bell was hanging, which possessed the wonderful gift of giving forth, whenever slightly touched, a clear ringing sound audible even at a great distance. In praying to God for deliverance

from her great trouble, she pressed the cross on her rosary fervently to her lips. The silver bell tinkled, and at the same moment a little barge suddenly appeared on the blue river. When it came nearer, everybody looked with astonishment at the strange vessel. Its form was light and graceful; but what astonished the people most was that it was not moved by either oar or rudder, but was gently gliding on the blue waves drawn by a snow-white swan. In the middle of the vessel stood a knight in shining silver armour.

Long golden locks emerged from under his glittering helmet, his bright blue eyes looked boldly over the crowd on the shore, and his hand held the hilt of his broadsword firmly.

The strange boat stopped just opposite the plain where the people stood motionless with amazement. The knight landed from the barge, giving a sign with his hand to the swan, which swam gently down the Rhine.

In silence and awe the multitude made room for the stranger who approached with firm steps towards the middle of the brilliant circle, and saluted the assembly with a solemn grace. Then he bent his knees before the Duchess and rising, turned towards Telramund, challenging him proudly to fight with him for the hand and dominion of Elsa of Brabant. The bold rebel's temerity seemed to fail him for a few moments, but gathering fresh courage he pulled his sword from its sheath with a loud scornful laugh.

The next moment the two knights darted at each other, their blades clashing in rapid strokes.

The whole crowd looked with wonder and amazement at the strange knight's great prowess. He parried the blows of his strong adversary skilfully. The combat lasted for some time, and neither of the fighters seemed to give way. Suddenly a subdued cry was heard, and at the same time the presumptuous vassal sank to the ground, pierced by the sword of him whom God had sent, and expired. A tremendous shout of joy burst from the gazing crowd, which rang from one end of the plain to the other and was echoed by the glittering waves of the Rhine. The people rejoiced in the victory, and thought that God himself had decided the combat in favour of Elsa.

The Duchess felt greatly moved. In her overflowing gratitude she sank down before her deliverer with tears in her eyes. But he bade her rise, and bowing low before her asked her to become his wife. She consented. What a heaven of bliss opened for the Duchess of Brabant! All her former troubles were forgotten.

Her gratitude towards her rescuer was transformed into passionate love, to which Lohengrin the virtuous knight, resdonded with tender adoration.

Yet though everything seemed now so serene in the life of the Duchess, there was a dim cloud which threatened to darken the clear prospect of her happiness. On their wedding-day Elsa had to promise her bridegroom that she would never inquire about his name, his home, or his descent.

Trusting her deliverer's honour and chivalrous bearing, she took the strange oath without a moment's hesitation.

Many years of bliss and happiness passed, and Elsa of Brabant hat strictly kept the promise she had made on her bridal morning. Their happiness was still more enhanced by the birth of three hopeful boys. They were their parents' joy, and promised to become in future shining ornaments of knighthood.

It happened however, when the eyes of the Duchess were resting with pride on her sons, that her mother's heart thought with grief of the solemn oath she had sworn on her wedding-day.

With how much more pride would she have looked upon her sons if she could have known them to be the offspring of a high and noble race. She did not doubt however that her beloved husband's lineage was a most noble one. Yet the thought that his sons might never bear their father's name, nor be able to add new glories to it, was lying heavily on her mind, and darkened the radiant image of her husband, that like a deity filled her whole soul.

The fatal question she had for so long withheld burst one day forcibly from her lips.

When she had pronounced the awful words, the proud hero grew pale, and freeing himself softly from her tender embrace, he cried out in bitter grief: "Woe to thee, my beloved wife and woe also to me! Now that thou hast uttered the question thou didst swear solemnly never to ask, our happiness is gone for ever. I must part from thee, never to see thee again."

A cry of anguish rose from her lips, but she was unable to keep him back. Waving his hand to her in a mute farewell her noble husband left the castle. He went to the Rhine and blew his silver horn.

Its sound was echoed from the shore like a long sob. The white swan with the boat soon appeared gliding gently over the river.

Lohengrin stepped into the boat and soon vanished out of sight and was seen no more.

His unhappy wife was inconsolable. Her grief was so intense that a short time after her health gave way, and she sank into a premature grave.

Her sons became the ancestors of a noble and distinguished race in the Rhenish country. Their badge is a swan.

The traveller who visits Cleves will still find a tombstone in its church with a knight carved on it, and a swan sitting at his feet.

CONTENTS

	page
Worms, The Nibelungen Song	5
Mayence, Heinrich Frauenlob	11
„ Bishop Willigis	14
Ingelheim, Eginhard and Emma	16
Johannisberg	26
Bingen, The Mouse-Tower	31
Castle Rheinstein, The Wooing	36
Castle Sooneck, The Blind Archer	42
Kaub, Castle Gutenfels	46
St. Goar, Loreley	53
Sterrenberg and Liebenstein, The Brothers	61
Andernach, Genovefa	72
The Drachenfels	85
The Monk of Heisterbach	92
Cologne, Richmodis of Aducht	99
The Goblins	104
Xanten, Siegfried	109
Cleve, Lohengrin	116

*

Druck: Joh. Heider, Druckerei u. Verlag GmbH, B. Gladbach